RISE BEFORE THE SON

ADVICE FOR SINGLE MOTHERS ON RAISING SUCCESSFUL BOYS

JENIEKA L. PEARSON

RISE BEFORE THE SON
ADVICE FOR SINGLE MOTHERS ON
RAISING SUCCESSFUL BOYS

iUniverse books may be ordered through booksellers or by contacting:

iUniverse
1663 Liberty Drive
Bloomington, IN 47403
www.iuniverse.com
1-800-Authors (1-800-288-4677)

Because of the dynamic nature of the Internet, any web addresses or links contained in this book may have changed since publication and may no longer be valid. The views expressed in this work are solely those of the author and do not necessarily reflect the views of the publisher, and the publisher hereby disclaims any responsibility for them.

Any people depicted in stock imagery provided by Getty Images are models, and such images are being used for illustrative purposes only. Certain stock imagery © Getty Images.

ISBN: 978-1-5320-7079-2 (sc)
ISBN: 978-1-5320-7080-8 (e)

Library of Congress Control Number: 2019904122

Print information available on the last page.

iUniverse rev. date: 04/10/2019

INTRODUCTION TO THE RELATIONSHIP YOU HAVE HOPED FOR, FOR YOU AND YOUR SON.

Transparency Reactive Theory

Building Traits:

- **Transparent** means: (of a material or article) allowing light to pass through so that objects behind can be distinctly seen having thoughts, feelings, or motives that are easily perceived.
- **Reactive** means: acting in response to a situation rather than creating or controlling it.

1. **Theory**: a supposition or a system of ideas intended to explain something, especially one based on general principles independent of the thing to be explained.

A set of principles on which the practice of an activity is based

An idea used to account for a situation or justify a course of action.

CONTENTS

1

THE BIRTHING PROCESS

Giving birth to my son was a very simple and successful process. "*Raising* my boy is the challenge." My son and I help each other out. You may wonder how "my son" manages to help *me* out. If you are, I will tell you and explain the growth that raising my boy **alone** has allowed me to see how powerful I really am. You see my boy doesn't realize, most of the time that he is teaching me every answer to every question that I may have on that given day about him. I **recognize** it and it makes the gift that much greater. Every day when I rise, I know instantly that I am either going to be a student to my son today or a teacher. Regardless he is going to get, mommy; the teacher or mommy, the student, no matter my situation in that present time and day. It is my responsibility to be aware and conscious of that belief, always, for the benefit of my son being raised by me, his single mom.

It was on a cold winter day, shortly after the Christmas day, that I gave birth to my son. My son is my first born child. I knew absolutely nothing about raising a child and to be raising a child that is a boy; I had no clue but what I did know was that I didn't know anything about raising a baby boy. I grew up in a household with both of my parents. My mother and my father were married and living together with two children. I always had my mom and my dad as a support system throughout life. I knew that the two of them together would protect me and my sister from whatever we faced. There was never a night or day that I didn't see the both of my parents and kiss them before bed. I often time would feel sorry for my boy because I knew that I would never be able to relate to him on his childhood level. The reason being was that I had both of my parents, with me, at all times. That was a fact that I never worried about growing up because there was always a sense of security and I knew that I would have my parents by myside.

Growing up I was raised in church and we lived a very traditional life. My grandfather was a pastor of several churches, so it was always known that the entire family would attend church every week no matter what came up. And we did. I became pregnant with my son in my 20's and I was not married; however I was engaged. At that time everything felt right. I saw myself birthing my son, having a husband and a family of my own. My story didn't quite turn out the way that I had intended it to, and I was ok with that.

No child ever asks to be brought into this world. They deserve to be treated as precious jewels no matter the circumstance. I believe that every parent has their own special bond with their child, and it can't be compared to anything else. The parent must be willing and receptive to their child to hear and understand their connection for that bond to grow. I held my tears back on several occasions and told myself, you will be the best mom that you can be. It was easy for me to look past some of what I felt like should have been different; but on other days, not so much.

I eventually sat down and talked to my grandfather about it and he being the traditional man that he was advised me that I should work the kinks out because he believed that only a man could raise a boy how to be a man in life.

I will never forget that sermon that my Grandfather preached and said that a mother could NEVER raise her son how to be a man. I knew that the sermon was for me, as I sat in the congregation with my 1yr old boy. It hurt me to some degree but I quickly got over it because that was not what I believed and felt from within. During that time, I did not realize that I didn't believe what my grandfather was telling me, however I accepted it because it was my grandfather. I always had feelings that made me at ease and prepared me for the mother that I am today.

I never stressed about if my boy was going to have a man in his life or not. I never felt the need to date and rush to be in a relationship with a man to look for a husband for the sake of my son. That urge was one that I never experienced. It was at that moment, after hearing my grandfather preach those words in the pulpit; that in my subconscious I knew that this would be a fight. Not a fight because we had two different views on whether or not a single woman could raise a boy or not but a fight because this is also what the rest of society believed. Well at least the majority believed the same thing my grandfather was teaching. I didn't know that this was how I was feeling then but it is crystal clear to me now. I was always a very bold and straight forward individual. As a child I was very vocal and knew exactly what I wanted and how I was going to get it. But, it was in a way that to me said, you will raise your boy to be the best that he can be regardless of what society would say or anyone else; including my granddad. I love my grandfather, I always have and I will never stop loving him. But, hearing that sermon that he preached, I believe was directed solely to me. It turned out that this was a blessing in disguise and for that I am grateful.

See, at the time I didn't know this. I just simply thought that maybe he is right. However, I pushed and I am still pushing today for my son. Every single second I am pushing out of my human self and into my spiritual self to be a better me so that I can be better as a whole for not just my son but anyone who I speak to. So, I am thankful to my deceased grandfather for that sermon. As I continue to push through to this day is a constant reminder that even society says that it takes a man to teach a boy how to be a man. That may be all well and dandy. I am not saying that it is not inaccurate information. I am however saying that this; to me, I believe to be debatable.

What I believe is that women can certainly raise her boy how to be a strong, successful, business oriented, goal driven, powerful individual. To me it is all what comes out of the mouth that will set the destination for our boy's future. It starts with us. Come go with me on the journey of why it so important for us mothers to spiritually connect to our boys to simply save them from the world. It starts with **us**, the mothers.

INSIGHT

The reason why I changed the way I thought as a single mother raising a boy was because I knew that my son could not and would not be any statistic of the trend that we see most of our boys raised by single mother's to be. I could not accept the thought that if I don't act on what matters, there could possibly stand a chance. I couldn't accept that and as a single woman raising a boy, my hope and prayer for you is that you chose not to accept it, also. There is no one personal hand book that teaches you the steps to follow as a single woman raising a boy. It is deeper than that. We must do some soul searching and that requires work and who in the world wants to work? The reality is that none of us really want to do the work however we want all the answers. Well I am here to tell you that until you do the work you will never have all the answers. However, this is the first step into helping you search your single woman soul to find the perfect way for you to raise a successful, professional boy. We know that there are going to be downfalls and we know that there will be trial and tribulations. Once we say that to ourselves, and accept that, we can then move to the next level of training ourselves exactly how to be all that we can be for our boys so that they make the right decisions outside of our presence. When we reach deep down in our heart and we look at this baby, this little boy that we birthed, that we brought into this world we must pay attention to the feeling. How does that make you feel? In what way does that move you? When we do this, we see all the great visions that we know lie in the heart of our boy. It is not until we allow our human selfish ways to get involved and disturb the atmosphere. We must learn to accept responsibility. We must learn to stop blaming the father for not being in the child's life. We can't change the father however we can condition our boys just the way that we see in hearts to do. We must stop being afraid of what already exist. What we must do is embrace it, forgive and move on.

2

THE CHOICE
IS YOURS

There is something unique about every single human on this earth. I believe that what we believe and what we see ourselves to be is who we will be. The **power** in "belief" for you is greater than any word ever spoken. It is the energy that you put into; to "know," that you have the power to do and to be anything that you desire in your heart. So, we are all different for this reason. Some of us will see the vision but fail to do the work, others will see the vision do the work and not have the faith put in the work, so it then never gets done. There are many ways that we think and believe in what we do and how we want to manage our lives.

When you start believing that there is no other option, for your son; you will begin to live your life differently than how you have in the past. Whatever the "knowing" is for you, you should believe that your life depends on it and do it! When you have surrendered all that you cannot possibly change, you will see things begin to manifest in your life, that you never imagined. You must let it go. You will feel the negativity energy begin to leave out of your body when you truly decide that this is not who you are and this is not how you want to continue to live your life.

I believe that every mother has at least one thing that she does as a single mother that no other single mother does. And this is special and you must take pride in yourself as a single parent. We may do things similar and we may think somewhat on the same level however; I believe, that there is no one mother that is completely 100% like another. We still, do have a lot in common. For example, if you are reading this book you are probably a single mother raising a boy or you know a single mother raising her son, in which, you want to help. Think about it, if all single mothers could come together collectively and bond with each other's idea's, can you imagine how much you would learn about other mom's and how someone else's "single mother" living situation may possibly help yours? Do you ever ask yourself what type of mother am I? If you have not I offer to you a gesture to ask yourself that question. What type of mother am I? The choice is yours.

Allow me to share with you the type of mother I am. I am a single mother. I am a mother of a very wise little boy. I am a mother of a black son. I am a working mother. I am a supporting mother. I am an encouraging mother. I am a mother of peace. I am a mother who is interested in learning from another single mother's. I am a mother who wants to grow, every day of my life. I am a mother who gets excited about tomorrow; another day to connect deeply into my son and those who are in his life. I am a strict mother, especially when it comes to his academics and structure in life. I am a protecting mother. I am a mother who will not allow anyone to tell me about my boy, unless it is him. I am a mother who recognizes success and I dig deep to be creative and find ways that will work for me and my situation to be a successful single mother.

Peace is my help-meet for me to maintain all the great qualities that I have as a mother. **Growth** and **gratitude** allowed peace to come in and save me. Just as I have mentioned, these great qualities that I have as a mother; we may all be able to relate in some way. And if we can't at first, I believe if we understand and study one another more; we will. We will find qualities that make you the type of mother that you are. We must recognize them and call them for what they are. For so long all we have heard, and understood is that ''we" as "Single" women could never, ever raise a boy to be a man. But, society never told us what we *can* do; society seems to only tell us what we can't do. It is ok, because I believe that it is never too late.

To go a little deeper, it will *cause* you to do the work. The tears will come, the pain grows, the anger will saturate and it all settles right in the heart of our precious sons and we don't even realize it. We know that there is a slight possibility that it could happen but we figure by then they will be grown, out of the house and on with their lives. Stop it! We cannot continue to live this way. Why do we do what we do, the way that we do? Is it *because,* we don't know any other way? It has never been taught to us and we just don't get it. (Especially when we are born into a marriage and raised by both parents, in the same household) Let's be true to ourselves, why would mom and dad teach us how to be a single parent unless they were one? It would make no sense.

I believe that all parents want to be optimistic and believe that their daughters will grow up with all that they need, including their husband to be there for her son. Single women, raising boys unfortunately have no way to tell what the outcome will be. The father may seem to know how to be a perfect gentleman before his son is born; however, he may not know the first thing to do or to say to make his child feel welcome and loved. Listen to the concept of that. The man will have all the answers for us while we are together in a relationship with him, for *us;* however as soon as our son is born and brought into this world, he does not have the capabilities and the qualities to say or act to his son what a father should be and that, eventually will cause depression in your son and a loss of hope for his future.

At some point none of us had a child. When we did it was a 1st for us in everything that we had to do for that child. It was our first experience; we had to do the work. We had to grow; we had to learn we had to build. Did we walk out because we felt that because we didn't have the answers, we should just leave? No. We stayed and we grew and we are still growing to ensure that our boys will have all the answers that they need to get through life, facing real life situations and knowing that they can conquer whatever comes their way. Why would my mother teach me how to be a single mom to raise my son to be powerful and professional if she never even had a son? We learn from models and examples along the way and at home. That doesn't mean that our life will be a model of what we learned. It is all a reflection of what we create in our boys and decide what we want our boys to see in us.

The process starts with us as mothers. We have more ability to create and prepare our boys to walk in the ultimate divine purpose than any other influence in their life. I tell myself what type of mother I am every day to remind myself of who I am. That is one question that no one else can answer but me. You know who you are as a mother, own it and if it is not right and you know it will not benefit your son, I would suggest to you that you reevaluate who you are as a single mother; all to save your son. I don't sit around and wait for someone to voice their opinion to me on what type of mother I am. Pay attention to your boys.

We as mother's often want to see our son's dad (or sperm donor as I call them) in them; which then reminds us of how much we don't like their dad. What we tend to do is, speak our boy's noncustodial parent's life into our boys. And it is usually of their dads. Not recognizing all that is taken place and building in our sons to be exactly the way that their father is. We will say things like "You walk just like your dad", "You act just like your dad." Now all of that may be like a certain degree, if we remember DNA and traits. I get that. However, we still have the power to build them up and allow them to become who they were born to be. Once our boys come into this world, they are already who they are and what they are going to be. All they need is guidance in the right direction to lead them into the role of success! Be careful of the things that you speak into your boy and his ways. It will sometimes back fire. This effect causes us to be angry with our own son for no reason. This behavior toward our son will eventually, set our boys up for complete failure in the long run. Let me put it to you this way. If we continue to say out of our mouths, to our boys that you look just like your daddy and you act just like your daddy…guess what… our boys will be just that. We all have heard more than once that what we speak is what will be. Whatever comes off our tongue and out of our mouths, are the actions that we will follow. It is quite very simple if you look at it from this angle. We tell our boys that they remind us of the very man that we despise. That we hate. And our boys know exactly how we feel about their dad; it is the energy that we give off about the situation. Depending on the age of your boy, he may not understand it completely, however; there is a sense of unhappiness that comes into their soul and it confuses them. They are then stuck between both parents, not knowing what to say or how to think. They are innocent beyond measures and at this point everything to them feels like it is their entire fault and they are left with an incredible pain that they do not know how to embrace the pain.

There are just some single mothers that will never reconcile with their son's father and they will never be able to openly and gracefully co-parent. I know that because I am one. My son's father and I can never seem to agree on anything. We have tried and we have talked and it never works. After so many talks and attempts you come to an agreement with yourself that this is one relationship that will never be healthy. It is sad and the fact that my boy is so bright, gifted and humble makes it so much harder for me to understand it. But I have learned to accept it and I must move forward for the sake of my son.

We always have choices in life. We as mothers must choose to do what is best for our boys. If you want your boy to be successful, you will change what you say to him and around him, and how you say it to him. Do what you must do to demand respect from your boy but don't deprive him from the trust that you need to give to him and show him that you trust him; and, the love. I believe that trust and love are very critically when we talk about single women raising our sons. We as mothers must be willing to let our boys lead at some point. This is where they can build trust. Are you willing to be that mother to allow her son to lead and trust that he will do it right? These are the kinds of questions that we as women need to ask ourselves to prepare a successful future for our boys. Once we begin holding ourselves accountable for the mistakes and hiccups that our boys made, we can accept it and move on. It is all a process and with any process there will be mistakes. When these mistakes come we must accept them and move on. We must be able and willing to stop blaming the father's for not being around.

If you really want to know the truth, you will begin to understand the father's not being there has absolutely nothing to do with how YOU decide to raise your boy. Women are the first love that her boy knows. She is the type of love to that boy that no other being could ever be. The reality is that we get to choose what type of mother we want to be. We have that ability. God gave us that perfect gift to make choices in life. We can be whatever type of mother that we desire to be by just telling ourselves the truth and walking into that role. When views are changed and you begin to focus on the predetermined outcome for you boy it makes being a single mom so much more understanding. There is no chart that tells us what we need to do to be the best mom that we can be. However, our hearts tell us all the time. If you reach down in your heart, and pull that information out it will be everything you every hoped for and more.

Search in your heart to find all the tools and the resources you need to make being a single woman raising her son a blessing. Because indeed, it is!

3

THE PROCESS: MOVING FORWARD

Mother's to their children are like GOD! We have all the answers to cure any physical, emotional or spiritual situation that our children face. Most importantly our boys look up to us to determine what characteristics he would want in the women whom he decides to one day is the mother to his children. That is a very complex decision. It could mean that our boys see something in us that despise and confirm to them, that they do not want some of our characteristics in the types of women who they choose to date when they are older. Or, they look at us and see how strong, powerful and humble we are; and choose to find those same traits in who they decide to be with for life. Whatever they decide, we must know that it will be based on what energy we feed to our sons throughout the time that we raise them up from the hospital to college. Mothers are put on the spotlight from day one. We are judged on how good of a mother we are and the situations that we allow our children to be a part of. Although, we never asked to have this kind of a spotlight; we find ourselves here on many occasions. It doesn't make if fair but that is where we are today. This is where we must make a conscious decision as mothers, and choose to create a positive energy and space for us to raise our son's; to ensure the healthiest environment possible. As a single mother raising a boy, we specifically must be somewhat more delegate to the fact that we are single

11

and raising a boy. The reason why I believe that this is the only way for us to think is because we are not men. Biologically, we have never been a boy and because of that, we will never know how to be a boy or a man. As mother's we must make the decision to accept this fact and choose to learn through the life of our sons. Although we are not men, I believe; it does not mean that we cannot raise a boy to be a man. The universe, GOD would not have made it possible for us to birth something so different from women that we would have to have a man present to raise him successfully. That to me is an Omen! We are mothers, nothing is impossible for us, if you believe. Once we open our minds and our hearts to believe that once we make the decision to accept what has been handed to us, we will begin to live a more peaceful life when it comes to raising our boys. It first is a thought and you must ask yourself a list of questions. For example:

1. As a mother of a single boy, am I willing to accept that it is possible for me to successfully raise my boy alone without his father present?
2. As a single mother raising a boy, can I handle the grief that will come at me when I am told that no women can a raise a boy the right way?
3. As a single mother, do I believe that I can hold it together because every time I look at my son I see his father in him?

These are just a few questions that will help you get to a place in understanding the mental things that you need for yourself and to help you transform into another dimension for the sake of your motherhood. Your questions may not exactly sound like the few that I have listed above, however; you must be honest with yourself to get the answers that you need. You want to be truthful and know what it is that is making you feel like at any moment you will give up on your boy and send him to be with his father or somewhere else. Understanding the situations that you face with your son, that will cause you to be frustrated or angry with him and his decisions are the situations that you need to focus on first. What does your son do that causes you to be very angry or upset with him? What are the decisions that he makes on his own that make you very proud of him? Before you begin to share this information with your son or anyone else, I want to offer to you to keep this information confidential until you are ready to grow with your son together on a new dimension.

It is part of the process that you keep these questions and the decisions that you have written down in a journal or your iPhone; as to why you may struggle with raising your boy and not accepting his behavior. This part of the process is very important because what you have made up to believe is true about your boy may not necessarily be his truth. Which then makes it unequal and you two will always but heads and will never be able to come to an agreement on anything that you try to collaborate on, ever. It will never work. That is why this information is important that you keep it to yourself in the beginning. You don't want to overwhelm your son and make him feel pressured into agreeing with you on this process. This theory will have to grow on him. Make the decision that you must learn to understand why you have a hard time seeing him for who he is and understanding his image.

Don't make his image about you. Often, we paint the image that we think is what we see in our son whether it is good or bad and we are usually wrong. I believe that often we struggle with seeing who our boys really are because we already have another image painted in our head about who he should be. The mother-son process, which is what this guide will teach you, does not suggest that we misinterpret who our son is and to do that we must work **together**. It will more than likely leave any mother sad, lonely and feeling like she has failed within her means to raise her son, being single; successfully, if she doesn't eventually understand who her son is.

The goal here is to get you to a point to open your mind, cast down the image that you see for your son and allow him to be transparent. Give yourself this opportunity to make the decisions about you and your boy's relationship privately and expect to explore **together** with your son and learn with him, who he is. There may be some things that you may not necessarily be ready for; however, it is all part of the process and it will be challenging in the beginning. It will allow you to grow through understanding and acceptance to get you to a level of truth for the relationship. Try this task and be patient during the process. All of this takes time and you must be open. If you have come this far in reading this book, you have already made your first step. **<u>Congratulations!</u>**

4

SACRIFICE FOR SUCCESS

What are you willing to sacrifice? When we think about sacrifice we find ourselves believing that we may possibly miss something that we really like or enjoy. For the most part that part of our belief is right. When we sacrifice we are letting go of something that we have allowed, time and space for, in our ways of life and we have become comfortable with the sense that it is relevant. The point of sacrifice should not be about a loss; it should much rather be about a gain in life.

In life, as single mothers we position ourselves to be the way that we believe is right for us. We practice this lifestyle and we perfect it. So, why in the world would we be willing and ready to make a sacrifice that will cause a change or a shift in our behavior? We have been taught to believe that if it is not broke don't fix it. What happens if the strategy is not working? Do we change it or do we go with the flow? To reap benefits that you have never seen before you must be willing to sacrifice somethings that you are comfortable with. That simply means living without what you are used to. When you begin to grow your family, you should be willing to grow and open your mind. When there is another life involved, often; as a single woman and we fail to shift ourselves into the arena that helps us grow; as a parent. For us to be able to adjust our minds and grow our spirit to understand who our sons are, we

14

must be open to the idea of sacrificing. I will be the first to tell you that if you are not willing to take the next step and fear losing; we have a bigger issue ahead of us than we may believe.

In my experience I had to take a leap. It was always a passion of mine to make sure that every day I find myself telling someone what I have learned for that day. Most importantly I made sure that I shared what I had learned daily with my son. It was a sacrifice in me taking the time to make sure that I shared the experience that I thought was so great with my son and to let him know that I was learning daily just like he was. It became an urge; a feeling and I had to make sure that I shared this lesson with my son so that he gets me. It was when I felt the urge to become Transparent with my son. That was just the beginning of what I was willing to sacrifice. You will find that it is no longer about you *all* the time and your son needs you, too.

I didn't quite look at it in the beginning as a sacrifice, because I didn't feel like I was losing anything or living without something that I was used to having. But, the more that I recognized what I was doing to make sure that my son understood that every day we should grow, I recognized that I was giving him a taste of maybe "mommy doesn't know it all." When we make the decision to change in behavior we must accept that our son will either see it the way we intend for him to see it, or he will simply come up with his own vision, interpretation and view it in a totally different aspect. However, that doesn't mean give up. We are "Mom", every child's life line; we must dress up in the "mommy role" which says that we know it all. How could let our son know that we don't know it all and risk the chance of them using it against us? We sacrifice.

We believe that we can't possibly let our boys know that we don't know everything and that there are still a lot of lessons to be taught to mommy and a lot for mommy to learn. Well, that is when we must take control and prepare for the shift. The shift will help us open and prepare for what we are not used to. Just because we are mom and we have total control over our children does not mean that we must deprive our sons of their human-being. I believe that we must show that we are just as human as or sons are and encourage them to know that we will mess up and make mistakes; this will allow our boys to see us the way that we want them to see us. Are you willing to give them that much power? It becomes power because we step out on faith and take a risk.

How would your son react if he knew that you were learning about life just the way that he is? Would he feel safe and comfortable or would he use that against you whenever you try to discipline him? There is always a downside to every upward situation. The strategy comes in finding out what is most important to your son, referencing you. This will all be new to him and to you because you have never put it in front of him like this before or even thought that this may work. It will all be a new way of thinking and risking a little of the power that you hold as a mother. To know if you are really making that sacrifice that you never imagined yourself making, you first need to ask your boy what he admires most about you. Go directly to the source, your son; ask him the questions that will help you strategically transform into not just a new mother but a new woman. For some, you may get an answer that he admires you for the way that you take care of the household, or the way that you love him. Whatever the answer is that you receive from you son, don't take it personal; that is the first thing. Depending on the relationship that you have already begin to build with your son, will determine the way he answers the question.

If you are the single mother that has a pretty basic, good relationship with her son; you can suggest that he may answer saying "I admire the way you love me." While that is all good, see if you can get him to go deeper with that. Ask your son to be a little bit more specific in how you love him. Because there are levels to the way that we love our children, and we want to make sure that our children are aware of the levels as well. If they are not, begin to teach them and show them different scenarios that make the love levels more noticeable. I will talk more on "The Love Levels' later in this book. On the contrary, if you and your son's relationship is a train wreck and on the edge of hitting rock bottom, you too have an idea of how your boy will answer the question when asked, "What do you admire most about me?" He may rebel and give you a negative reactive approach or he may soften up because you never bothered asking him, and give you the answer that you least expected. Take the risk.

These questions will help you build a more solid idea of what your boy is lacking and what he is hungry for. Often the help that we need and look for; years at a time is found in a simple question directed right at the source. It is an approach to the next level. Always give your boy a point of reference that even when you are not his best person in the world, there will always be a thought or a moment so powerful that he has of you to make him remember why he admires you the way that he does.

We must be willing to plant those positive thoughts that our boys have of us rather than giving them any excuse to think otherwise. This is very delegate at the beginning, because this is the foundation of which you will begin to build on. Decide what you are willing to sacrifice. Ask the questions directly to your son and allow him to answer them without your input. It is also important that you let your son answer "your" question with his own answer. Don't make him feel like he needs to give you the answer that you may want to hear or else your foundation is distorted before you get it up off the ground.

Write the answer down in front of him to give him a sense of how much his answer means to you and to let him know that you are serious and you want the relationship to build and grow. Let him know that you need him to answer from his heart and that you promise not to judge his answer or even speak on it. The only thing that you need to do with your son's answer is accept it and right it down. Remember acceptance is key. After you have received and accepted his answer as to what he admires most about you, take that answer and review the question and the answer daily until it sits so deep into your heart that you dream of it at night. Make the question and the answer so relevant in your life that it begins to manifest in your spirit. If you truly want to change what is not evolving in the relationship that you have with your son; take the risk, ask the questions and don't go to bed at night without looking at the answer that was given to you from your son.

5

REMOVE THE VEIL: THE BLESSING IS UNDERNEATH

How many single mother's do you believe every imagined in their mind, while giving birth to their son that, they would be an alone, raising this boy all by themselves? I never imagined it. Although I never imagined it, I have accepted it and I am comfortable with it. I accepted the fact that I am a single mother raising a boy.

When I could talk about who I am as a single mother raising my son and do that with grace, integrity and dignity; I had overcome the most difficult challenge that I had ever faced! I knew when I begin to hear myself talk about what I do as a mother and how proud I am to do it, I had truly accepted the fact that I am in this alone as a Single woman raising my son. Ready for next, is what I call it.

You will know once you are ready for the next step in your relationship with your son. He will look different to you; you will see him different. He will become transparent and it will be a mutual thing. His walk will be different, his talk will be different.

You must get past the **"what if's"** and focus on the **"what now's."** With recognition becomes responsibility and some of the times we choose not to recognize what is because we simply do not want to take responsibility. We must own it. We must take responsibility and allow ourselves to be surrounded by other single women who want to make the change, who want the best for their boys and will not take anything less. The hard part is acceptance. We weep at how our emotions take on certain things and that is not unusual. This to is a process much like many things that may come up. In some cases life throws us lemons and someone once said "If life throws you lemons; make lemonade!" It can be done.

You will be amazed with your transformation all to make better decisions for your son so that he can have the best future possible for him. You must get it in your mind that you want the best for your son and nothing less. You must tell yourself every day that my boy will be powerful, successful, respected and brave because of me. Be the model to your boy that he needs. Stop dwelling on what should have been and focus on what is.

I believe that everything that is purposefully for you, you will receive it. What may seem to be not going your way or not so good, will eventually be grace and gratitude to get you to your success with your relationship that you have with your son. I also believe that we have the power to mold, shape and create uniqueness in our sons, if we simply focus on what we want for them. It is not a curse it is a blessing. Now some of us may feel like this is a generational curse and we accept what we feel and the fact that it has been passed down generation after generation. Why? Why can we accept, what we feel, is just a generational curse and not accept, that, our sons father doesn't want to be a part of his life. I want to help you understand and focus on the situation for what it is. We are what we believe. We all have heard this at some point in our lives. We create in our lives what we believe. If there is a trend in your family with single women raising their sons and for whatever reason you feel like this is a generational curse, let it go. Break the cycle. Remove the Veil and free it.

Stop feeling sorry for all the women in your family, who are single and raising boys and some of them may not have been as successful as other's. And, some may have failed. That should be enough for you to say that enough is enough and know that our sons need you, no matter what the circumstance is. Surround yourself with other like-minded single women who refuse to give up on their boys. There are many of us like this, however; unfortunately, there are more single women, who are successful in their businesses and in their careers but just don't feel like they have the courage, patience or commitment it takes to raise their son and be successful at it. This doesn't mean leave them abandoned at a young age or walk out on them at birth. What that means is that by the time adolescence kicks in they are simply not willing to do the work. And then everything that has been taught "A man is the only one to raise a boy" comes back up in their lives and they feel like giving up because deep down inside of it has been instilled, that being single raising a boy will never work. So why do the work? And then we give up.

This is not the way. If we see this for the blessing and not the curse we will raise far more successful boys than criminals or drug addicts and drop-outs. We as single women raising our sons must take ownership of our boys. They belong to us. It was the women that carried them in our wounds and birthed them through trimester, labor pains, etc. We have already won, and now it is time for us to acknowledge it. The blessing is the Son. The blessing is in us as single women, and that is what we should focus on.

We as women are the nurtures so we already have everything that our son could ever need. When they fall and get hurt on the playground, they run to mommy. When they get their first girlfriend, they run to tell mommy. When they are ready to take a girl to their first prom, they run and ask mommy. Mother's nurture and make everything better; this is what we are called to do as women. So why we would believe that as single women we could never raise our sons to be successful. It is not true and we must not accept that we cannot do it. But, do we accept that we cannot do it? Or do we just accept that because the father was not around, our boys will head for self-destruction and that it will not be our fault. I am here to tell you that it will be our fault.

It will be your fault because this son belongs to YOU; their dad did not birth them YOU did. We as women are the nurtures, this is what we do. This is the gift that we give back to the people that we love; even to those who we struggle to love. It will be our fault simply because we hold the GPS to our son's destination. We have the power and the ability to create whatever we desire for our boys. if you want your son to be successful, you will change your thoughts and take ownership for what is yours. It starts with YOU!

We have every tool that we need to create a desire for our son's to be successful. However, it is up to us to introduce the tools that we have for them. If we never introduce them to the resources that we have for their future and give up on them, because they made one bad decision; yes, they will fail and it will all be because of our lack of willingness to take responsibility.

Own it. This is the only way that it will work. I had to make up in mind that I did not want to be the type of mother that set her son up for failure. Whether we want to admit to it or not, what we choose to introduce to our boy's will ultimately impact their lives, careers and future in one way or another. We must be reminded that males in general think on a totally different level than we as women do. So, what does this mean? This means that every model that we introduce to them and every behavior that we show them must be followed up with a reasonable explanation. I know you may be saying I don't own my son any explanation, I am mommy and what I decide is what it is. That is correct. I am not saying that your judgment should be questioned by your child; however, what I am **promoting** is that you make sure that your boy understands the behavior or the model on his level, because he will never understand it on your level.

Stay focused on the big picture. He will never understand why his dad made the decision to not be a part of his life. That is one aspect that he will never understand but it your responsibility and your duty as a single mother to make sure that he learns to accept it. Just because we learn to accept something that occurs in our lives at some point does not mean that we get it. It does not mean that we understand why. There would need to a very good reason as why his father was absent in our son's life; and even after that, we still may not be able to comprehend it because our thinking has changed, our responsibilities are different. We may never be able to lower our thought process to be able to understand why they chose to do what they do and did and that is ok if we accept it. We are not accepting it for the father and his insecurities we are accepting it for *our* own **healing** and our **power** to give our sons the tools that they need in every walk in their own life. This has nothing to do with the father it has everything to do with us as single women raising boys! We must be aware that there are just some things that we will never understand. Learn to accept that it is not meant for us to understand other's choices, decisions and actions. That is all normal. Maybe the blessing is that it is just not meant for us to understand it or that if we understood it, we could potentially open our heart to receive more negative emotions and it will make the healing process that much more difficult. I say; leave it alone and learn to accept, that everything is not meant to be understood; but we have the power to build and create anything that we desire for our sons so let's start now. We must protect our heart (which is like a garden) from any negative focus that could possibly enter our minds to cause us to lose focus on the blessing. This again is the beginning of the process and it will be hard. When you make up in your heart and decide in your mind that you will not let your son go and that he needs you, it will be a smooth process and it will all work in your favor. The blessing was given to you so embrace it all, through the good, bad and indifferent. Nurture the blessing so that your son will win in the end.

You are not alone. There are many of us in the exact same situation. We are hard on ourselves because we always feel like we have failed simply because:

1. We don't have a man.
2. We are left alone to raise a son.
3. We try to understand why.

We live all our lives in misery believing that we have failed and this is the way that it is supposed to be and we are not supposed to even think that for one minute that we can change it. We easily accept that we will never understand but we very seldom want to accept that we can change it. We suffer the 3 things that I mentioned above and we believe as though we have failed. We run from the truth and we hide from our sons so that we don't have to tell them the truth because we can't accept the truth. And then we dream and wait for them to turn 18 years old so that we can ship him out, send them to school or simply tell them, "You are grown now and you have to get out of my house." We think that is the way to teach our boys to be strong, and powerful, and we feel like a burden has been lifted off our shoulders because now they are no longer under our roof and we can "Get our groove back." As a reminder, if you ever lost your groove, you didn't have one to begin with so stop with the fantasy, accept the truth and listen.

We take the blessing and do whatever we want to do with the blessing. That is not the way it is supposed to be. The mistake is made when we begin to think that it will all be over when our boy turns 18, they are grown and we no longer must deal with them. This should make you said. This should hurt your heart. Instead you should remind yourself, that he is mine, my precious gift that was always a blessing in a disguise and whether I saw it at birth or whether I am just now seeing it, I will get it right for him. We say things in front of our boys all threw their childhood, adolescence, and pre-teens that they hear and it affects them in the long run. They hear us saying these mean things about their dad they don't understand and we will turn around and take everything out on them. We should take responsibility for our own actions and stand up and do something about it. We set our boys up to be the way that they choose to be whether we believe that or not. But we have the choice.

Often time we spend all our time telling our sons what they couldn't do, that we forget to tell them what they can do. When we fail to tell them what they can do, we fail to introduce them to the possibility that they can be successful, that they can be whatever they desire to be. We keep those valuable tools from them and wonder why they never have the will to do anything other but to be just like the man that walked out of their lives without explanation. This is the type of behavior that will cause us to create an angry, fatherless, sad little boy's. We tell them that they are supposed to be strong and tough and that they are not supposed to cry and that if they cry they are weak. We must stop pulling life out of them slowly and start breathing life into them deeply, and we do this by being intentional about the words that we speak to them and about them. This will sit and live in the pit of their stomachs to want nothing more but to desire to be the best that they can possibly be. With hope it can and will be done.

6

THE LOVE LEVELS

Raising any child is a challenge for anyone and when you evaluate; a mother, who is single and raising a son, the dynamic shifts and there are a lot of potential hiccups that will come into play. This does not mean that you must struggle to figure it out. What this means is that we work on forgiving ourselves and assuring that we are complete and hold as an individual, so that we can work continuously on raising our son. There are levels raising our sons successfully and the Levels of Love that we give and support them in.

The process can be painful but anything that is going to work successfully must go through a process and there may be pain. The pain is not because we are single; the process is painful because we don't understand why we are in this situation. When we don't understand something, we make it up in the way that we analyze it in our minds and that usually is from the way that we have experienced what we felt in our hearts. We hardly ever try to find a positive answer to why the man of our son decided to walk out on his life.

What if we knew and understood everything before it ever happened; there would be no need to grow. We don't allow ourselves to accept what is. So, what we do is we suffer through the pain; we never accept that we are even hurt for our sons, which influences the bad behavior to act and say according to what we feel. When we feel pain, we say hurtful things to our boys about them that cause them to rebel and be angry. We may not see this behavior in them right away but what happens is that the information that we feed them through our negative behavior resonates inside of them. It becomes a seed that we have now planted in their heart and in their minds. They hold on to these words, and they act according to our words. Most times we are given signs and I like to call them "Red Flags", it is up to the mother to catch them and act according to the red flags.

I could recognize the red flag that was shown to me and I knew immediately that I had to surrender to the anxiousness and the guilt and the pain that I endured and held on to simply because I couldn't understand someone's flaws. I couldn't understand why my son wanted so badly to debate with me every time I tried to correct his behavior. It was almost as if he didn't trust my judgement and everything that I said he had to come back at me with the complete opposite. I was frustrated, I didn't understand what was going on and I felt like I just couldn't take it anymore. I told my boy to call his dad and he can go debate with him because I was done. Let me just say that was a big mistake that I made by putting my son off on someone who clearly doesn't want to have any parental responsibility. During that call that my son made to his dad; this sperm donor begins telling my son that I was incapable of knowing and understanding what to do or say to him but to be tough and he will be alright. I immediately grabbed the phone and hung up. I looked directly into my boy's eyes and apologized, immediately. I had to apologize to my boy because I saw the look of confusion in his eyes through his tears. He was confused not just because he has never understood why his dad is not in his life; but he was confused that I would ask him to reach out and call someone who simply does not want to be a part of his life. That was the red flag. It was definitely "Grace" that came over me and allowed me to see the red flag grab a hold to it, confront it, bless it and let it go.

We must be committed that we cannot put our sons a situation that may come across as if we do not have the patience to understand them and that we will call the next adult (father, grandma, etc.) to let them figure it out. When we knowingly see that we must step up to the responsibility and own what is ours we can begin to heal and let go of what is not meant to be. We cannot sit and wait for our sons "sperm donor" to catch on to reality and get abroad the ship because it is now sailing. Think about it, what if that day never comes when he decides to jump aboard and see what great works his son is capable of and learn who he is a person and understand his ways?

The power lies inside of every single mother and to recognize omens and unhealthy situations is just one tap away from you. The signs are always there and sometimes we ignore them because we are scared to face what we see as pain. No one wants to face pain and tackle it so that we can move forward in life but it is the only way that we will be able to get to the next chapter of our lives. Once we accept the pain and push through it and **bless it out of our lives**; it can never come back. We release it like a helium balloon that floats into the sky and is gone forever. Once the releasing process has truly taken place we begin to walk into our purpose.

Things will become clear and the wisdom to understand more and more of the challenges and obstacles that you may be face with; will make sense and you will know how to approach them. Utilize the positive energy as the power to do exactly what needs to be done for our sons as single woman. We begin to tap into that strong power and begin to make a difference about how we think, walk and talk and it is worth it.

As mother's we are always on the go to make a difference for our sons by any means. We act off our own emotions because ultimately, we want to save the day ("Super Mom"). Once we have conquered the day in us on world we look to be appreciated it for it. We look for recognition from the one person who does not care, and that is the father to our son. We often time remind them of all that we have done in their absence. It is all emotional and when we don't receive the praise that we feel that we should receive and this can cause anger. Tapping into your inner power will enable you to not look for recognition or confirmation from anyone. We should set our expectations and leave room for error up based on the acceptance of the truth. This will help getting over the situation easier and safe. We learn how to prepare ourselves mentally, and maturely to whatever comes our way. We are not suppressing or ignoring we are now conditioned that every fight is not our battle and so we pick and we choose. Women are nurtures and the same way that we nurture every relationship and every encounter that we face we must do the same with our pain. It allows the pain to turn into pleasure. It is the power from within that will allow the pain to convert to a different pleasure and peace.

We will do all the things that we are destined to do for our sons and not look for recognition. And this is perfectly fine.

Understand that we must raise our son explaining to them the circumstance instead of criticizing them for the outcome. When we embrace the fact that we are single women raising sons; mentally our minds take on a paradigm shift and the energy level is powerful. The power already lives in us. We become stronger and wiser, and spiritually prepared for our purpose.

We have been taught and know pain to be uncomforting and hard, and no one wants to bear pain. However, we want greatness. The key to getting greatness on all levels of love; whether it is conditioning our son or anything else is accepting that there will be pain and to get to the next chapter you must just release and accept any pain that you have had.

No one can fail you mentally, but you. Your idea of what is right is the boundaries to each level of love that you choose for your household and your son. That is not an open invitation for anyone to come and change that. Failing will then not be an option in your home because you are now in control of all boundaries on any set level and you will show your love through the boundaries that you have set for your son.

The pain is the root cause of the greatness. The pain is the key to opening greatness. The reason why we can't plant the seed of greatness in our son's heart is because we have not accepted the pain. We lie to ourselves to cover up what other's think we have done wrong. In most cases **we are not** the reason why we are single and left, trying to raise a son. Technically, no one is a fault. But for some reason Mothers are blamed and judged on so many different levels which will cause us to believe the blame and accept it and then we give up and fail. Our family members criticize us for being a single woman raising a boy, our community will criticize us because we can't teach our boy how to be man, and social media will point fingers in our direction because they feel as though we don't have the resources that we need to develop a brave man. So, we listen to the non-sense and we accept it because everyone else accepts it and we feel we may as well join the band-wagon. And once we accept and settle with all the "nay-sayers" every wrong thing that could possibly be said about a single woman raising a boy, we act out. The behavior of a Single Mother becomes altered according to what we hear and our ability to accept the non-sense. That is not the way we are supposed to be. If no one is fighting for you, then you are going to have to fight for you. We are so willing to open and accept what is being said about single woman raising boys however we are not willing to accept the pain that it is causing us. We agree to what society is saying about single women and their "attempt" to raise a little boy with no father figure around. We blame the father of our boy and because he is not around we take it all out on our son. Sadly, our son has no clue why his mother is so angry with him and why he feels like he is not loved.

We can't change the DNA of our children however we can nurture their attributes. We know and understand one's DNA to be the fundamental and distinctive characteristics or qualities of someone or something regarding a person in which we cannot change. This is true. We understand it, we get it and we accept it. Someone could never change one's DNA. Often, we feel and excuse our son's behavior based on what we believe is the DNA of their father. We feel like we can never change it, and this is the way that it will always be because it is in their blood. Once we accept this fundamental fact we never work on anything about the situation that we are faced with. We are not willing, because we don't believe that it will change. Therefore, it is important for women to make a commitment to become wise in thought and move the focus from the DNA to the physical traits we may be ready to decide what "right" needs to be done. When we talk about their "trait" we understand a trait to be a distinguishing quality or characteristic belonging to a person. We also know a trait to be an attribute, which is better known as a feature. The trait we can inherent, the DNA is what we are born with. When we begin to accept the greatness that lies in all of God's children we will study our boy a little bit harder and a little bit longer to set the example and increase the attributes in him that he has already inherent from you. Accept who you are and why you are a single woman raising your son. Get to the core issues of why you are the called one to raise this boy as a single parent.

When we stop looking at the DNA and begin to look at the inheritance we have now mentally opened our minds and spiritually opened our hearts to accept the purpose that we have on this great earth to raise this boy to be the most successful, professional, brave, aspiring individual that one will know in his own unique way.

We have had it all wrong for years. Our perception never allowed us to see the progression because we viewed it backwards and now we must change the way that we view our situation. We are single women raising boys for a purpose not a mistake. We all have the exact same thing in common and instead of us embracing it, we deny it. Stop giving the father all the credit. We do understand and know that all credit is not good credit. When we blame the father for not doing what we think that he is supposed to do we enable them to a certain level of credit; whether it is a good credit or bad credit, it is credit. With credit becomes power. So not only are we enabling their credibility we are giving them power and control over who we are as Powerful, single women. It speaks to the fact that women are not worthy to do the job in raising sons; that we are not fit to teach a boy how to be a man and it limits our abilities that God has already given to us as nurtures. This will cause a draw back within the Mother-Son bonding process, because it implies that as mothers.

The good news is that the only one that can get your power back is you! And the way to get your power back is to accept the pain, let it go and grab a hold of what is yours and that, is the ability to teach your son how to be everything that he desires and hopes for. Talk your son; build a relationship with your boy, which nothing or no one can ever come in between. The hard part is over and that is the birth of your boy, now the purpose is ready to take course and explore and accomplish. Begin to view yourself as an accomplishment; a desire to evolve and to grow through self, own the accomplishment wear the accomplishment, believe in the accomplishment and know that you are the accomplishment because in your heart you believe more than whatever it is that took control of your power that you can raise this boy to be the very best. When you say this to yourself you must believe it. Sometimes we must remove our inner abilities from our minds. We often time get so confused by what the mind is telling us, what our hearts are saying to us, what our spirit is calling us to be and what our human being tells us we want.

It seems like a lot; however, if we focus on the bigger picture and that is; that it is not us it is our boy we will begin to see life and the experience in a different walk. If we didn't have the pain we wouldn't have a purpose. We wouldn't have a purpose to get up and fight for our power back, we must believe in this. We have the right and the ability, to move and live through our divined purpose in raising our boys. When we accept the pain, we open our hearts up to believe in the power that rest inside.

Think to yourselves on that precious moment when you gave birth to your boy. All the negativity was removed from your mind, your soul and your heart because all that mattered at that time was giving birth to a healthy baby boy. You had control. It didn't matter to you if you were getting along with the sperm donor at that time or not. It didn't matter to you what was going to happen between you and the father to your son. The only thing that mattered in that very special moment was you laying your eyes and wrapping your arms around this precious seed, one that you gave birth to. I don't know of any proud mother to say anything other than positive comments at the time of birth. Somewhere between the pain and the denial that we are in pain we lose it. We lose the control and power; we lose what we thought we had but the reality is we gave it away. Unknowingly, we gave our power away. That doesn't mean that we cannot take it back; because, we can. Anything that we once had we always can get it back. Especially, when we unknowingly give it up; not internally but externally because we listened and accepted the put down that society has said about single women raising their sons for a long time. So, now to get the power back we must do the work and fight and of course as I mentioned before, no one wants to do the work, so we settle. We accept what is not originally the way that we were destined to be and to keep everything simple we lie to ourselves. When we lie to our own souls we become angry because now are we not fighting the simple egotistical thought that we could never raise our son to be successful, we are battling and fighting our inner abilities that wants so badly to explore but instead we keep them hidden behind the pain that we never accepted to keep from facing the hurt, which is the truth. We must come to an agreement with who we are as a person and who we are as a mother.

As a person living for just one, not really having a commitment to be a model to someone or something we get tangled up in the things that don't necessarily matter. We can act wild and crazy, we can use bad verbiage and not care who has heard us say these things. This matters to some but not so much to others and if that is the way that you would rather be, then it is you and only you to make that decision in your life. However, when we are called to be something so gracious and perfect in the eyes of your child, that should be one of the top 5 reasons why you are willing to fight, why you are willing to live, why you are willing to have the ultimate power over your boy; because nothing else matters to you than to make sure that your boy has all the knowledge you can possibly give to him both spiritually and mentally. We as mothers need to remind ourselves that we must do what matters. When we begin to do what matters rather than the things that don't matter, we will get a different result. The pain lies beneath the surface, it has found its way to sit deep down inside of **"self"** and call this place home to where you don't feel like you want to do what matters. All you want to do is care for your child and send him on his way so that he can be out of your way so that you can live again. **No!** It will never be what you anticipate it to be because you never faced the pain, removed it from your heart and set it free. So now you are concerned with only you; when will find a man; how to advance your career, etc. and all that may be humanly obvious but I am here to tell you that won't work to the best because deep down inside you are still faced with the same pain, the same insecurities the same lack of power that you have had all along and no man is going to be willing to stick around for too long to figure out what happened to you along the way and the marriage will fail. It will be a cycle of unhealthy relationships for you and unhealthy relationships for your son because you didn't want to fight to get what is yours. This is what will be created and eventually hinders you, from all your greatness if you don't own up to the pain, accept it, bless it and release it. Acceptance is simply acknowledging the fact that you are hurt and not living in denial. You accept what is and you will face it to get what is waiting for you and that is the biggest gift of them all which is your blessings. Acceptance is also simply making yourself aware of what is. In most cases as women we see the red flags and we know that they are real but we don't want to acknowledge them. So, we ignore all the warning signs making us aware of what is headed down the wrong path and then we are mad at everyone around us because we fail to accept and become aware. We do this because we want to paint a picture to our family and friends that we have it all together and we can't even accept the pain that the father to our boy doesn't want anything to do with us or his son. We never get over the reality. We make that reality so powerful that it becomes a feeling and we continue to allow ourselves to suffer in the pain of what we can't change. This should matter to us. This should make us want to push through the pain because we care not just about our happiness but the overall success that we want for our sons.

This is what matters, and therefore we push through the pain to get to the purpose to live in peace. It is all about what matters to us. Make those things relevant that really matter to you. Do what really matters. We don't have to continue to lie to ourselves and the people around us any longer, because we know what is and we know what we want. When we can grab ahold to what is and what we long for, it will make knowing what matters relatively easily and we will fall right into our purpose. We don't have to be afraid of the pain; the pain does not define who we are. What defines us is that we can recognize the pain, live through it to conquer it, bless it and set it free. Once we bless it and set it free it will never come back because at that very moment when you decide to bless the pain and release it; it no longer matters. You are then healed from the pain that you have endured for so long because you didn't know how to accept the pain and push through it. I do believe that every boy loves his mother beyond words and unless we give them the listening ear that they want and deserve from us we will never know it. All our boys really need from us is clarity. When we make it clear to them that no matter what happen between their dad and his mother, it will never affect the relationship that a great mother and son can have; and the admirable relationship that is destined. When we can look our boys in their eyes and let them know that they matter and making sure that they "get it." This is what really should matter to mothers. You will watch a flower (son) bloom like you have never seen before. Our boys need clarity! We as mothers owe it to them to explain. Don't look for daddy to explain to your boy, why he left or why it didn't work out between you and him. That is not the clarity that our boys need. The clarity that they need is really simple and it goes like this: "I love you and I will never leave you, I will be here for you every step of the way. Speak to the negative thoughts that could possible rise up in your son and explain to him that If you get a thought in your head that someday I may walk out on your life for no apparent reason I want you to run to my arms and tell me you are having those thoughts and we will talk about them to release them and we will move forward." That is the type of clarity that your boy needs. **"Reassurance!"** And the only way that you can be that example and model to your son that you are destined to be; is to accept the pain, bless it and release it. You may have given your power up but don't you dare think that you cannot go and get it back. It is yours. No one can work your power the way that you can. I want you to accept your power and believe in your power. It is yours.

7

PROCESS AND PATIENCE

Often, we like to believe that we need somethings yesterday. Do you ever stop and pull yourself out of that obnoxious thought and ask yourself, why? How often do you tell yourself that you are pleased with whom you are and you will not accept **mediocrity** and you *will* strive for success every day of your life? If you're answer to the question is, never; reading and studying this book will improve your thinking and get you to a place where you can **transform** into a better mother, parent and person so that you can be a better parent to your boy. We have created and instructed our minds to do exactly what we tell them to think and believe and in turn the mind tells our heart how to behave, and we follow it. There is no such thing as we needed something yesterday. We may have wanted it yesterday; however what good would it have done for us because we didn't have the preparation to even know how to handle it if we would have recognized it the day before. The message that I am offering here, is to be intentional of everything that we could ever want and everything that we will ever need, we already have it. We already have the ability, the tools, and the power to get whatever it is we want if we only acknowledge it. So, the process does require **patience**. The patience is not in waiting on what we need to come to fruition; however, the patience is doing the work to recognize the thing that we are looking for lies in our heart. **We must do the**

work. When you think of a process, think of order, strategy and guidelines. You can also view it as a "process" or a step in the right direction. For you to go through any process that you set yourself up for in life; you must develop a sense of patience. Train yourself to follow a process and set goals that are attainable for you to accomplish. Some of our process may be very similar to one another and others will be slightly different. Whatever the process you decide to follow, it is important that you stick to it, or you will waste the gift that is in the process.

Raising boys and being a single woman is already a process. If you step outside of self and look at the big picture you will then be able to dissect "what is" and begin to understand what you are facing. Patience is the number one necessity when I think of process. **Process requires not just patience but focus** and long-term goals. To get this right, we as single women raising boys must train ourselves how to make this work in a very selfless manner. Baby steps will be the introductory to the process and your patience will be tested. The result will be a huge reward, but we must stick to the plan and follow whatever process that we set for ourselves and our son.

Examine yourself and focus on all the surroundings, (people, places, etc.) that you encounter and make a choice. You may find that some of your choices will require you to make some sacrifices in my life but if getting the process started means letting some things and people go for the sake of a mother-son bond; it must be done. My offer to you is **"testing tips"**, while following the process. We are all striving for the same goal in the end and that is to raise successful, business oriented, polite little boys to be their very best.

The testing tips that you will find in this chapter is more like a cheat sheet to be a single woman raising a son. The tip of the iceberg is how we can challenge the process to make sure that our boys are smart, intelligent, successful, and respectful and all the other great attributes to make them the best at whatever they chose to do in life and to be family oriented as well. It can be done. As women raising our young boys to be men we have all the power that we need to be successful at this. The tips are actually very simple. But, it is how you apply them which is what makes it work or not. If you follow the process that is drawn out for you in this chapter, you will be very impressed at yourself and the art that you have now created. *Tip #1, **Believing** in our hearts that the process is simple and easy; everything else will fall into place and you will be amazed. We must remember that being

conscious and always intentional that whatever may be going on at that very moment **"don't panic."** When we panic we become unintentional and the mind begins to work at a speed so rapidly that it takes complete control over the body and it then becomes what other's like to call "an outer body experience." Do you remember back in the day people saying your mind will play tricks on you? Well it is true and if we are not careful the mind will take so much control and it will simply bring you down. It may appear that the mind is full of negative thoughts. I am here to tell you dear, that **it is not you**.

Your heart does not have an ounce of negativity in it. *Tip #2, **Listen to your heart**. The patience comes solely from the heart. It is the closer to your inner self than the mind is. We must know how to **become in tune with who we are;** *Tip #3. We are mothers; single mothers at that. We must know how to make patience a priority and not let anyone cause us to panic in whatever situation that we are faced with. It is the patience that will keep our hope alive. It is the patience that will build our strength and allow us to act through wisdom. Practice being patience and listen and compare what your mind says you want and what your heart tells you what you need. Remember patience is about waiting on what you want to happen but that does not mean that you forget to believe in what you want. It is all a process.

*Tip #4, **Train your heart how to talk to your mind** instead of your mind talking to your inner self you will be amazed at how easy life will be. Become addicted to what feels easy, much like breathing. You have the power to control every situation by allowing the heart to take control, remove self, not judge and let all that you may disagree with pass right by without having any effects on the person you are. As single mothers we must make up in our mind what it is that we choose to believe about ourselves. We should set boundaries with ourselves and everyone **connected** to us. Becoming mad at a situation that didn't work in your favor causes frustration and stress. We use these types of situations as baby steps to learning patience and understanding that to win we must fail, first. Let it go and keep going. **Look deeper than just thinking**. It is so much more to thinking beyond what you have ever expected in life, it will be a life changing experience. Trust the process. To trust the process, you must have patience. To have patience you must trust yourself that you are making the right decisions about what you want to happen for you. Know your worth. We are worth so much. The role that we play as far as single mother's raising a boy is an **advantage**. We are born winners. Find your niche and take charge. Not just anyone can do the job that we do daily successful. Instead of coming home every day pouring a glass of wine because you feel like you barely made it; come home every day and pour yourself a glass of wine to celebrate yet another day that you accomplished everything that was set out for you on that day. It is truly a reward. **Embrace it**.

8

LISTEN TO HEAR
WITH YOUR HEART

Often when are boys are trying to tell us things we listen to respond, when we should be listening to hear what it is that is on their heart and that they want to share with us. Listening a little while longer and allowing that patience to come in and settle into the conversation, the dynamic of the conversation changes and in fact your mother/ son relationship begins to grow. Even when it seems that our boys have other important people in his life to talk to; that doesn't matter. Our boys are going to find it most important to come and tell Mom. It is a natural human need that boys carry and we must accept that. In fact, all mothers should be so proud, happy and thankful that their son wants to take the time out to talk to her and let her know what that day's experience was like. Many of these conversations can prevent suicidal thoughts or any other violent crime. Making a difference is possible, but first let's learn to listen to hear and not always respond. If we are not able to recognize them for the way that they are created, we most definitely will fail. When are boys talked to us, it is something deeper than just the point that they are trying to make. Patience should come into play and with them and give them the time that they deserve. Remember, again, they run to us before running anywhere else. But, if we continuously reject our sons, who is it that they will run to? We are their hero, and we are the answer to all their fears. Let those facts stay in your heart and at the very front of every conversation that you have with your son; you will begin to open and hear so much more coming directly from his heart. I always believed that there were differences between **listening to someone speak and hearing someone talk.** It is easy to hear someone talk, that is just the sense of hearing. However too actually listen to the words that are coming out of a person's mouth; is on another level and we must understand and accept that to get to the next step in raising a successful young man. We hear our boys talk all the time but when will we begin to listen to the words that are coming out of their mouths. That choice is ours! This is another **power move** that we already own; we just should claim it and recognize the talent. It is never too late to tap into that side of motherhood and activate the gift and watch everything in your mother / son relationship begin to unfold. If you think that it would be helpful for you and your boy, practice listening exercises. Have fun with it. Make it a routine. This is a process that the both of you will experience together. That is what makes it so worth the while because while you get to teach him how to be successful like you, you also get to learn thinks about your boy's character that you may have not already known.

The key to knowing if you are following this process correctly is that you look for things in your boy that you have never seen before. That is when you know that you have evolved in this journey with your son and you now have accepted the power to raise your boy just the way that you feel he deserves; to make him the best that he can be for himself. Regardless how we listen or hear, it usually will cause some sort of reaction. Therefore, the skill needs to be perfected or it will be a constant battle. We as single women raising sons tend to want to correct everything that they do and say. But on the contrary we want them to grow-up, man-up, or just stop acting like a baby. Some mothers will even tell their son's that showing their emotion and crying is not acceptable. This is when the foundation is broken because the foundation is that they are human just like we are and they have emotions and need guidance, too.

If your son comes to you and have a conversation about his day, his teacher, his coach; whatever the case may be listening to what he must say; if there was a conflict, test your boy and see if he was able to come up with a conflict resolution by himself. If he could, of course you always want to applaud that type of behavior. The key thing in this situation is that you want to avoid correcting him or telling him he was wrong. If you see something in how he handled the situation that was improper, of course mention it to him but you want to suggest it instead of telling him how he should have handled it. This is very important. Remember that they are coming to us to tell the story because they have a sense of pride about it and they want you to feel the pride in them also and to be proud for them. Make it as easy as possible for your son to talk to you. It is nothing more important than allowing your boy to know that he can come and talk to you about any situation and you will help him in every way necessary. The listening process takes time and it will probably be the toughest while you and your son go through this transition preparing him now for the rest of his life. You all will grow together and you will feel so empowered and grateful to have such a son.

Our sons may sometimes feel like we are not for them 100% and it is because we are not willing and listening to them 100%. They don't necessarily now that we are not listening; they just know that much of the time a conversation is had it never ends up positive. That can sometimes cause a rebellious spirit and it makes much more friction and chaos in the atmosphere between the mother / son relationship. It is the listening process that is going to make the relationship or break it!

Our sons are not going to adjust to who we are and our character. That is not their job. It is up to us the Mother to make sure we are flexible enough to know when to bend and in what **direction**. We must know how to adjust for the growth of our sons. Struggling with this acceptance is likely and making it right for you son to be successful is a big deal. If you feel like you need to go and seek counseling; there is nothing wrong or unusually about seeking professional guidance to help you better the relationship that you have with your son. I know that this is not going to happen overnight and it may not even happen in 90 days, but it will happen and it will work in your favor. Everyone has a past and not all our past has taught us how to pay attention to the way that we respond to certain situations and even our children; especially our boys. As professional, successful women we have now recognized that it is more to the story than us, just birthing a son and being his mommy.

Sometimes we want to think that because we feel like we work every day we feed them, put a roof over their head and all the necessities; that is, it. That is how we like to teach them to survive and anyone can do. The **goal** is to teach them how to be successful and listening to every word that comes out of their mouths is the first step into making this a success. We can master it. There is so much power in listening as it is in silence. Because when you are listening, chances are that there is a sense of silence and content and with every word that is coming out of our son's mouths we will hear and listen to their heart with our heart. We will be willing to act accordingly from the genuine, innocent place in their heart that will teach something new about them every single time. Seeing the genius in him, and everything else that will follow will make it all worth it. The process is amazing if you just believe it and listen to it and allow it all to fall into place.

Explain to your son that this is a new journey for the both of you. Let your boy know that while he may not see the work, you are constantly working hard for him to be great at everything that he touches. Our words mean so much especially to our sons and we must tell them something great every day. Sometimes our boys already feel as if they will never be successful in life because the fact their father has already walked out, they never had an opinion about the situation and they should deal with it when they were never even give a choice. When we begin to open our minds, and listen closely to the words that our boys are saying, it would make sense to us why they can never understand anything that we tell them. If you haven't been through this phase with your son, trust me it is coming.

We come to a place where everything that we tell our sons, they either admit to it not understanding what we are saying or they shut down simply because they don't understand but they don't trust us enough to even begin to tell us that they do not understand. Going through this as a single parent is hard and it will cause a lot of weight if this is not addressed. This type of behavior from our sons can be handled properly and "professionally" and it will work for the relationship. It is not our sons fault because they don't understand what we mean when we explain something to them or if they don't understand why we made the decision that we made about any situation that caused them to be affected by that decision. It is NOT their fault. I have heard several single mothers raising boys say, "I don't have to explain nothing to him"; and the reality is, is that we don't. We don't have to explain anything to our boys or give them a reason behind every decision that we make on their behalf but we should because this will make him feel included and like he is a part of you and the decision-making process. Once we shift our **behavior** and **believe** that we as single women have the power to bring our boys to successfulness; we will make life so much easier for our sons and they will be more than likely to grow up and know how to make the right decisions and walk away from wrong situations that may come their way during life.

Remember, it is all about **what the single mom is willing to do**. These adjustments must be committed to and acknowledged daily. It is a **constant fight**. The reason that it is a fight is because **society** makes it that way and because we are the minority. Being women, we will always have to prove ourselves to the rest of the world. So, if we take that information and look at it very closely, we have women as minorities, raising our sons to be successful. The odds are against us. The focus must always remain on our sons. We already have the **power** to operate in grace and control. We can do it!

9

THE POWER IN FIRST STEPS AND TIME MANAGEMENT

What is the first step that you will take to open yourself up to receive and accept exactly who you son is called to be? The next step would be supporting his decision. This is a challenge because it is causing us to step out of our comfort zone, the things that you are used to and do something different. It can be done if you believe it and want it for yourself and your son. Once you get that in your spirit the rest will come natural. Critical small steps toward a bigger purpose will always out-weigh the discomfort. Hang in there and see it through.

If you are the single mother that constantly has the sperm donor calling you, harassing you, belittling you and always putting you down as a single mother and you accept that; the first step for you is to stop accepting that immediately. Do not tolerate that behavior from your son's dad or anyone for that matter. I know that it is easier said than done but you will get through this. You are not alone. Take the time to take an hour of your day (if you are a working mom this will work well on your lunch hour) and go somewhere where the environment is different and just become one with yourself. **Sit alone**, turn your phone off and any lines of communication (only for an hour) and take the time to just focus on what you are faced with at that there moment. Become mindless. Stop the brain from thinking negatively and force positive thoughts to come in. This will help you listen to your spirit instead of you talking to your spirit, telling your spirit how you feel, what you need, what you have and what will happen next; **this behavior will help you listen**. Sometimes when we listen to our spirit we already have all the answers that we were looking for and it will change our lives permanently for the good. Continue to try this behavior at least **7 days straight** before you decide to take the next call from your boy's dad. I call this the **transformation stage**.

During the transformation stage, you want to stay humble and positive. If you don't have to answer your phone, don't. If you can get away with not reading or responding to your personal emails, do just that. I know that if it is business we can't cut that off but we must continue to stay focused on the transformation stage. For some 7 days may not be long enough and for others, you may not need 7 days; however, I recommend seven days. Drink plenty of water. Pray often during this time. Please don't misunderstand that process. Pray to God, of whom we serve. Whoever you talk to that is above you in this energy filled forced universe, that is who you should talk to doing this process. If you can get away from television, remove it for a short time. When you get home from a long day and you and your boy are together, talk to him. I would suggest you listen to him and let him talk. Change up the routine. If you cook super, allow him to help you even if he is not up to it. Do his homework with him and this time give him all the answers (just for one day). Remind him that you are here for him and **you have his back 100%,** no matter what. Let him see you doing the things that matter. Say words to him that matters at the very moment. During the transformation stage **we are teaching ourselves to only do what matters**.

Ultimately, we want to come to a place where we can live our lives doing what counts, long term. Who wants to live their lives doing the things that "don't matter?" We always have a choice. So, I want to offer to you, do what matters! If arguing with your son's father every day is what matters to you, then you keep doing that. If that doesn't matter, end it now. When you feel like you are in the moment and you are allowing yourself to transform, even if you get off track, immediately be reminded that you are transforming. Correct what you may be doing wrong; then you can have that first conversation with your boy's father and set those boundaries with him because you have corrected and healed the wrong within yourself. Let him know that there will be no more of the negative behavior excepted. He no longer has the right to mistreat your intelligence and you will no longer give him a free pass to do so. **It starts with you**. The transformation stage is in progress. And eventually he will see it and not even have the courage to address you in any other way other than in a positive and a respectful way.

The transformation belief of your mental state is acknowledging that you can overcome the hurt, by letting go of the pain and knowing that truly deep down inside you have done all that you can possibly do. If the pain is coming because your boy's father left you (for whatever the reason is) and you feel like you all were made for each other, was meant to be together and want to continue to fight to make it work; you will not transform and you will find yourself suffering and stuck in a position that you don't want to be in. Although if that is the type of mother who you are and you want to continue to search and keep hope alive for the relationship that you think you have been deprive of with your son's father; the choice remains yours.

You should be willing to let go of what you do not have and will never have and embrace the fact; and then you can turn around and embrace your son's needs and transform your spirit into believing what you never may have imagined before and that is finding peace from within. **The transformation state** will come in all different forms for all different women; however, you must believe. You will be wasting precious time if you tell yourself this is what you want and then turn around and decide, **not do the work**.

The challenge is **changing your atmosphere**; for at least an hour a day. Allow yourself a silent moment to just embrace, and accept everything in that moment at that time. When you get into your car, before you crank it up, stop… Stop to take a minute and breathe and focus on the power and control of that very moment that is presented to you at that time. Listen to the birds, the rain, the cars, the sirens. Whatever you are faced with at that moment take the time to recognize what it is to you. That is what the work consists of. Don't get caught up in the "I am a single mom, I am too busy to take a minute; type of way." That is not the type of mother you are. And if you were, it is ok because this is your key to getting to the next step in bettering yourself, your son and the relationship between the two of you. Take control, you have the power to do so.

Sometimes we get so caught up in always moving and we never stop to just focus on the power that we should change whatever it is that we are faced with. When we do these things, our thinking process begins to take complete control over our lives and it is not always positive and if you are not careful, you will get lost in the negative thinking. Once this happens it really becomes more intense and difficult to overcome. Take the time to breathe through the transformation stages and the process will go smooth and the transition will be successful. Allow yourself to **vision** whatever it is that makes you happy, that **gives you peace** that allows you to accept even the things that you do not understand. Remember, acceptance is necessary to surrender and let it go. If you can remember in previous chapters we talked about accepting even the things that you will never understand. There is a **purpose in acceptance.** You may not see it at this very moment, however; you will see it if you **believe that you will see it**. Believing is seeing. It is the process to getting what you deserve as a mother and knowing you stand for as a single woman raising a son. All the lessons that you will learn from my writing are followed by the work that you chose to do.

The next step is asking yourself if you can complete the work. Only you can answer that question. No one can predict or tell you what amount of work that you can do but you. What will it be? You may ask yourself an even more challenging question and that is **where will I get the time to put in the work? This** is the biggest challenge question of them all. Being a single mother, we wear several hats. There is always other work that should be done and we feel like there is no room for anything else. Mostly we feel the need to devote our hard-earned time to our employer before we give it to our household. I have been there. We feel that it is imperative that we cater to our employer to the best of our ability because that is who keeps food on the table and the power on. If I may, I advise you to not short change your home for feeling like this is the only way to live. I am not saying quit your job. I am simply offering a suggestion to begin making baby steps towards greatness, peace, comfort, and forgiveness. Give yourself a schedule and stick to it. It is all about **time management**. You have the power to design your day that every day is successful. The goal here is to not just survive; it is learning how to be **successful while surviving**. Anytime we change the way that we have been doing something for so long, it becomes uncomfortable. However, to get to a comfort space and place of peace we must go through an uncomfortable experience for a short while.

We often lose focus and we find ourselves not following the plan to success that we have given ourselves. It happens. When you feel like you cannot go on, pick up the useful tool and read, study the words and the processes. Every process takes time and work. Nothing transforms overnight. **Set a deadline** to focus on one small thing in the beginning and you will be well on your way. You will know how challenging this process will be by the way you set your first goal. Set realistic short-term goals and then progress from there. For some, time management is not an issue; however there challenge maybe in following through or completing a project. You must be serious and you must be ready to make a complete change in your life. Don't settle for what you have now. Keep digging and grinding from your core to get what you deserve and your son will follow your lead. When we push ourselves, and strive for nothing but excellence, we are planting that seed of excellence in our home and in the people around us. Most importantly we are planting it in our boy. **This step is not a fight**. This is simply a reward that you are giving yourself, recognizing that you are on your way to be the best single mother for your son that you can possibly be.

Your plans for yourselves are gifts. Nurture your plan and **work on it every day**. When you are tired and feel like you cannot go on, take the time to look at your plan while you have forced yourself to relax and listen to yourself breathe. There is always time to do the things that we want to do. Trust your plan. Pray for your plan and watch it unfold like never. Share your vision in your plan, with your son and **ask him to hold you accountable**. This will also help the two of you build a stronger relationship in goal setting and planning. Talk about this journey often together as mother and son and explore all the greatness therein. Explain to him that you are doing this for him. You will watch his soul light up like the brightest star in the sky. Our boys need our attention. They want to know that we need them. Make them feel useful and encourage them to be a part of this process with you because it is for them as much as it is for you. We are working to better ourselves as single women so that we can build them up as successful men. The only way that we can do that is through perseverance, hard work, dedication trust and patience. Once we have mastered these, everything else will fall right in to place. You will shock yourself and others around you. The power of time management will change your life forever

10

HOW TO HUMBLE YOURSELF THROUGH IT ALL

The Universe talks to us all the time. It is up to us to recognize it, listen and act on what it is telling us. Often time's we find ourselves in a situation that we feel like we don't deserve to be in; both positively and negatively. The reality is that we don't deserve a lot of **great** things that we have, and we still find a way to manage and enjoy them. The importance of learning to humble ourselves will allow us to excel to the next level that we are called to in life. However, we must choose to recite a mantra, pray or worship; it must be done. It is the ultimate way to humble your life so that you can see those things that are before you that you would not be able to see if you are not humble. Be silent in the humbling process. This will help you learn to **wait (patience)** for not just the key to being humble; it will also allow you to wait for the answers to many questions that you have.

The first belief in humbling yourself is that you must believe that there must be a decent order and a firm process. And in "order" to have order there must be "obedience." When you have the obedience, to structure the order, all the opportunities that you really deserve will literally greet you every morning when you first open your eyes and rise.

11

IGNORANCE IS NOT KNOWING / KNOWLEDGE IS KEY

It takes patience to understand and digest a child's psychological, physical and spiritual emotions. As parents we should listen to instruction to gain knowledge in areas that we lack. Even as parents, we were not born "a parent." Which means that we should condition ourselves how to be the best parent that we know how to be (which in most cases is knowing only what we see) and pray that what we think is the best; our child will interpret that attitude into their behavior and live a life that we would want our children to live and that is the best. Unfortunately, there is no law book that guides us how to parent to our child. All parents are faced with challenges with raising and caring for our children on different levels in life. The parenting level that we are speaking on in this book is obviously the Mother and Son level. There are multiple levels within the Mother and Son level. Some levels are more extreme than others but we must acknowledge first that parenting is a challenge. It doesn't matter whether you are married, single, widowed or divorce; there are challenges that you will face at some point along the way with your son. Once we can accept the challenges and understand that it is normal; we are well on our way to helping us improve our attitude and the behavior's we pose as parents. Opening to learn on all levels will elevate you and the relationship that you have with your son.

Our **attitude** and **behavior** that we give to our sons has 99.9% effectiveness on how they will respond to us as mothers. Some adults wear their emotions clean on their face and although whatever the emotion is whether good or not; your child will know if it is towards him. The damage in wearing our emotions is; because our Son's know immediately if what we are feeling is directed towards them; when we express happiness and it is not towards them they feel not wanted, not loved, and unable to please mommy. When we are angry, and they know that it is not towards them they feel ignored, pushed off, left behind, blames and feels not as important. Whether the emotions we wear are good or not children have a way of seeing through us without us even knowing. Let's just say our boys know certain things but cannot necessarily communicate or express the things that they know about their mom. Also, let's be honest, how many mothers do you know who sits around and wait for her son to tell her the type of mother he feels she is being to him?

Being **transparent** with you child, voluntarily will help you and your child **communicate** every emotion that you are feeling as an adult. It will prepare you for what's next. This process, is called **"Transitioning to become Transparent."**

Making a transition in any area of your life is a total **commitment** and you must be willing to sacrifice things that you may have never thought you would ever have to give up. But the important thing is that you know the sacrifices that will be made are a move in the direction to both **self-improvement** and parent growth. We never imagined that we would need to take up a career in child psychology to figure out how to be a successful parent and raise a successful boy. And although we don't, sometimes it sure feels like we can't win at the journey. Don't give up and don't lose hope. Most times we **do** have to pay attention on the psychological portion of our boy to ensure that we **understand** what they maybe or, are feeling. The way that we do this, is through learned experiences and behavior; making a commitment to transform our thought process and practice living a fruitful life. We must bring forth the fruits of the spirit for them to show up in our sons. We must practice; Kindness, Love, Joy, Peace, Faithfulness, Goodness, **Self-Control** and Gentleness. This will help us to live a peaceful and successful life and I ensure you that if these techniques and tools are followed your son will be more successful than you could have ever imagined. If you are a person who journals, etc. continue to write a daily reminder to yourself that these are the fruits that you want to bring out in your character. Use daily reminders in your cell phones all the time to be reminded that co-workers are watching, friends, family and most importantly your children; so, always no matter what, allow your character to reflect the way that you really want people to see. Eventually once this has become an ongoing practice it will become an **unconscious** attempt and it will be much like breathing and everyone around you will win. They will see the fruits that you bare and feel the energy that you bring and before you even open your mouth, they will be willing to trust what you say. In the mist of you making the sacrifice and committing to make a lifelong change in your character to better you as a mother to be a better person for your son; he will feel the changes in your attitude and it will become contagious. He will see that you have calmed yourself and allowed the atmosphere in the home to be peaceful and that is what he will breathe in and we all know that **what we breathe in we let out.** This commitment will be successful, the sacrifice is meant to be the result that you have looked for and waited for a long time. This is when you must **trust** the process and be patient. You may be a mom that never raises your voice at your son and may even feel as though you are already calm; however maybe your boy may need a little more voice from you and **another source of energy** other than calmness all the time. Because there are definitely different levels to parenting and because we are all made different in our own way, no one will do it the same. Once you can recognize that you have the power to create the life that you want for your boy, you will be open to learn and listen to ways and techniques that will teach you how to do so. Some mom's may carry a doctrine's degree at the highest level in law or medicine or in any other field; however, she may find herself single with a son, raising her son alone and not necessarily being the most successful at it. To those mom's that may be living it this way, it is ok; you are not alone and if you find yourself reading this guide you are well on your way to learning to revise your parenting **skills** and grow from where you are today to where you want to be tomorrow, and this book will help you get there.

12

LEAVE YOUR DEFICIENCY OUT OF THE PROCESS

Most, if not everyone has at least one **flaw** that may have caused a learned behavior in a negative way that could have caused unusual behavior in his/her character. The importance in **understanding** is just because we as single mothers have certain deficiencies, we cannot take it out on our boy! The key is to eventually get to a point as a mother, as an individual; to be able to put those behind us and not let those **deficiencies** control our behavior. We cannot allow our issues to be the problems of our boys. It is unfair to the child and it is not **honest** as a parent. We find ourselves sometimes holding our own self accountable for someone actions when indeed it had nothing to do with us. What happens when we take **responsibility** for someone else's actions? It causes us to be **distracted**. And therefore, we are unable to see our own progression and growth. In fact, it also allows us to ignore everything that we have already worked on to move in a direction of peace so that we can give our boys everything that they need to be a better them. In this part of the process it is very important that as a woman we surround ourselves with those who are going to bring out the growth from within. You will not have to question a person's presence or what they are able to offer to you. You already know without a doubt that if a person has your best interest at heart and will not provoke you to act out of who God has called you to be. At times it seems that it is so much easier to complain rather than giving thanks for being alive. I believe that we find ourselves complaining about what should have been or what needs to happen instead of being thankful for the idea to make things better. And when we have like-minded people surrounding us with those same deficiencies; we may never get to a place of **forgiveness**. Pay attention to those who are in your circle and surrounding you daily. It is ok to let some people go that you may have known for 20 years. If the one person that you have known for 20 years is not helping you push away from any distractions that you have about you or anyone else; it is time to let that person go. I understand that this part of the process may be easier said than done; however, it is time to put yourself first and say good-bye to the very person that you feel like you love the most. Just because we say good-bye to someone doesn't mean that we do not love them anymore. It just simply means that we are willing to grow at a capacity that does not invite everyone, even those you love. If the love is **reciprocated** by the other person they will understand your growth and let you go as well. **Growth and Progression** should always be the focus when are working towards pushing those deficiencies behind you.

Once you can silence your deficiencies you will begin to hear those needs that your boy is crying out for; however, you may be missing them because of your own distraction caused by your flaws. The goal is to accept what your deficiencies really are. If you are in denial and cannot identify your flaws but you know you have them, I would like to offer to you that you speak to a superior, a mentor, a relative; who you trust and you know they have your best interest at heart. If you are **patient** and **trust** the process, trust me it will work out and begin to unfold to be as peaceful and loving, more than you have ever imagined. You have the power to make it happen. Admitting that you have flaws and you have ignored them during your parenthood, does not mean that you have failed. The best thing about this process and any process is that there is always room for growth. You will be willing to accept growth every day in whatever form it comes to you in, if it is **growth**. The growing process will never get old and fade away. It is a **lifelong** experience. It will allow you to want to be transparent to your son and allow him to be transparent with you. Understanding that there are somethings (flaws) that we would rather not discuss with our sons; it is ok and we don't have to. The importance is that we can own it and grow from it ourselves. Some of our flaws are just simply not for everyone to know; however, when you are able to admit them to yourself you have made a **huge leap** into the direction that you want to better yourself as a single mother raising a boy. With that you can consider the race won!

Printed in the United States
By Bookmasters